Going to school

Written by
Tapasi De

Illustrated by
Suman S. Roy

I wake up
at 6 o’ clock
every morning.

Then I brush my teeth.

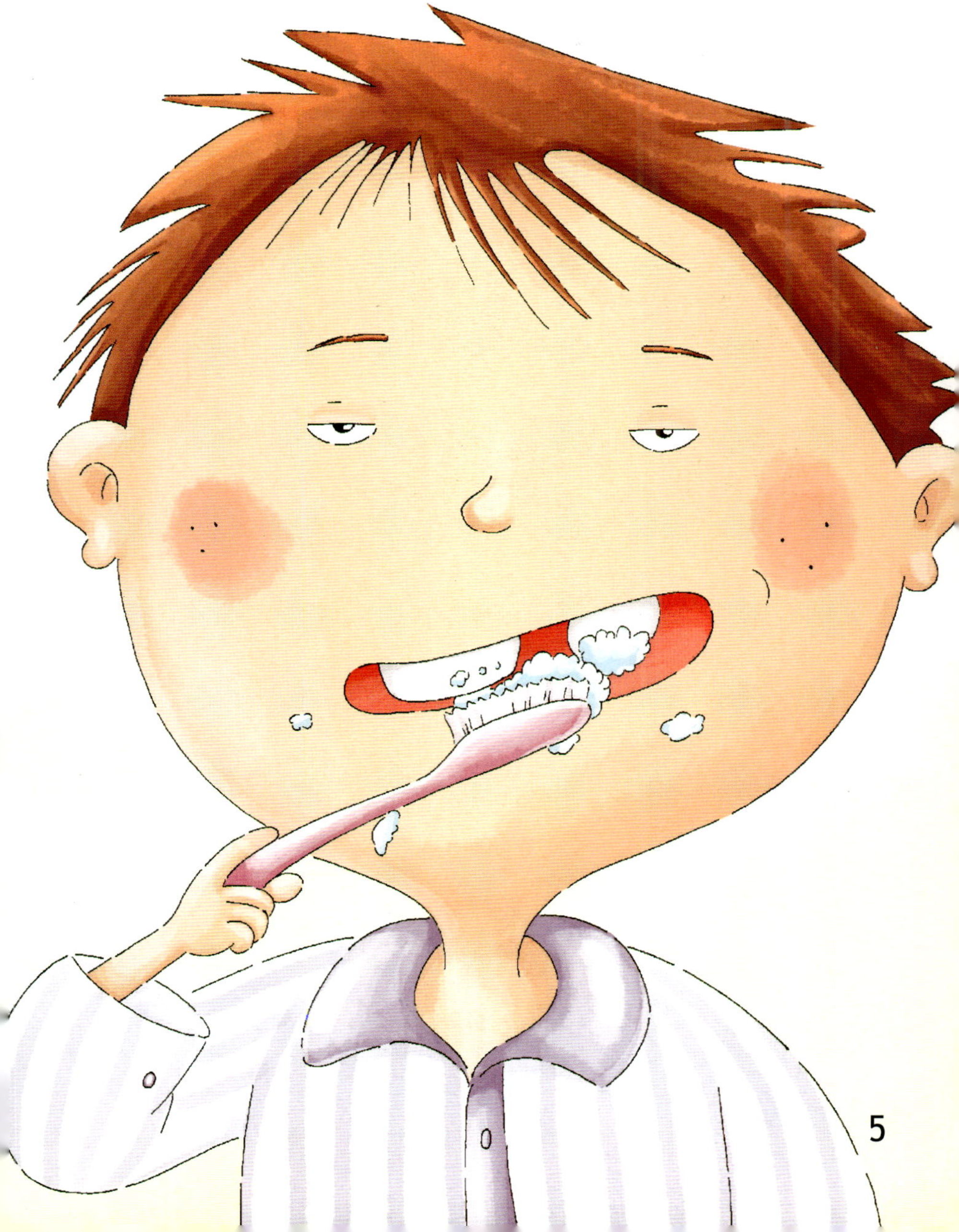

After that I
take a bath.

Next, I wear my uniform.

Then, I eat
my breakfast.

And finally, I wear my shoes.

Next, I pick up my bag.

And then, I go off to school!

I walk down to school.

In the classroom
I study.

At lunch we eat.

After the school is over, I come back home.

SCHOOL

I do my homework.

I love to colour in my free time.

In the evening
I study.

Let's spell new words

school
bag
teeth
brushing
drawing
writing
lunch time
walking
classroom
studying

home
wearing
uniform
waking
bathing
colouring
picking